The Chicken War Chronicles

By Larry Gauthier

| Corporal Ben | Lieutenant Dan |

Contents

Dedication

Preface

Chapter 1: The Nazi Invasion

Chapter 2: The Allied Japanese Tunnel Invasion

Chapter 3: The Ogre Prisoner Transfer

Chapter 4: The Search for Mike

Chapter 5: A New Chicken Commander

Chapter 6: The Korean Chicken War

Chapter 7: The Dark Screaming Zombie

Chapter 8: The Coal Mine Mountain Horror

Chapter 9: Finding Low Heaven

Chapter 10: The Squawk Hoppers and Angel's Choir

Chapter 11: Who Dan Pollock Chicken Disease

Chapter 12: Floozy Chicken Female Disgrace

Dedicated to my girls: Natural Born Chicken Fighters

Coal Town Family Children

Private Jack   Private Pig

Preface

The stories that follow are childhood reflections of the author, whom was raised in a small town in Missouri. The original town was built around a coal mining operation. As the mine played out and closed, the town faded away. The name of this town was Coal Town. When the railroad moved in, a new town came to life about a mile away from where Coal Town once thrived. Most of the younger people in this town never knew anything about Coal Town, but the author and his family remember the stories told to them by their Father. They lived next to the mining operation in a home built by their Grandfather. A large family; money was tight and they raised a lot of their own food. Raising chickens to put in the freezer every fall, kept the family in food through the winter. With extra money being scarce, there weren't a lot of toys. The children instead made up their own games and adventures to replace the boredom of daily chores. The task of raising and butchering chickens and other livestock was part of sustaining life on the farm. The imagination of the children replaced the daily chores with adventures; each task became another step in those adventures. The mother, made sure the children were raised in a Christian home. The father was raised Catholic.

The Nazi Invasion

The Allied Chicken forces pressed forward, helping the Nazi's to gain the Fortress stronghold (barn). The Coal town rebels fought back, armed with firecrackers, masking tape, corn cobs, BB guns, sticks, wire and numerous makeshift weapons. The rebels found that if you capture chickens and wrap masking tape on their heads so that it shaded the eyes like a visor, the chickens would constantly duck down like they were trying to walk under a board. The chickens were running in their crouched position just trying to get under the board which gave the rebels the edge they needed to capture the haystack.

The rebels fought their way back into the Fortress, sustaining numerous injuries, but all minor. The haystack was in sight, if they could only get behind that wall of hay, they would be protected from the onslaught of poultry slaps, and spur gouging. Lieutenant Dan let fly with a corncob, "smack!" he had struck a blow to the head of the Chicken Commander. The Chicken Commander was stunned; staggering around like his legs were made of rubber.

This commotion flustered the Chickens and they began to spur and slap each other.

At last the diversion needed to slip past the Allied Chicken forces. The Rebels pressed forward, the haystack was only feet away. No! Another devastating blow cast upon the rebel forces, a "Tiger tank" (turkey). The rebels knew fighting a Tiger tank was all but impossible without the aid of the 1st mechanized artillery squad (Archie and Bruce the dogs).

Lieutenant Dan was the highest-ranking officer of the rebel forces. General Lee and Colonel Jim had been shipped off to war on other shores. Lieutenant Dan had only Sergeant Ray and Corporal Ben to rely upon to get the job done. There was the Field Marshall (mother) but at times Lt. Dan was not sure if she was on the side of the allied chickens or the rebel forces.

He did however know that if an allied chicken crossed her, he was the same as cooked. At times she would send down an order to sacrifice a couple of the prisoners of war.

Corporal Ben and Lt. Dan carried out the unpleasant task of decapitating the prisoners.

Back on the front line, Lt. Dan called for assistance from the artillery squad (sick em) the 1st mechanized artillery squad jumped into action. It was working; the Tiger tank was being driven back. The Allied Chicken Commander had regained his senses, and called for the Tiger tank to pull back. Artillery was no longer effective; Lt. Dan called for a cease-fire. The Rebel forces; were right back where they were before the Allied Chicken Commander was wounded. The Rebels needed to come up with another diversion fast.

Sergeant Ray had been working on a plan, let's pull up the .50 calibers (BB guns) and snipe a few of their troops. We can make a hole in their line and slip into the safe zone (haystack). All of the Rebel forces took careful aim and pop, a hole in the line. The Rebel forces were back in business; they jumped into action and pressed toward the opening they had created. Feet to go, now inches, dive! They slipped into the crevice between the haystack and the barn. Oh no! The rebels did not know that the Allied Chicken Forces had called in their Asian allies (spiders), Ninja's everywhere.

This situation went from bad to worse; the rebels now had to fight their way out of the Ninja trap.

The rebels knew if they had to leave the protection of the haystack to avoid being devastated by the Ninja's, that they would be slaughtered. Allied chickens on one side, Ninja's on the other.

Lt. Dan knew he had to think of something fast, or the rebels would be goners. Flame throwers! (Railroad flares) Lt. Dan yelled pull your flamethrowers and blast the Ninja's.

The Ninja's crumpled under the blast of the flamethrowers, now to get back to fighting the Allied Chickens. It was time for bravery, no more inching forward. The Coal town rebels had just watched the new military weapons and tactics instructional video (Rat Patrol). It was time to devastate the enemy, no time for cowardice, take no prisoners. The Field Marshall had sent down the order it was time to fill the freezer. Lt. Dan had always felt the Field Marshall had been on the side of the Rebels, now he was positive. The Coal town rebels shouted in unison "Pluck them Chickens" the events that followed were total chaos, and will never be released to the public. All the public needs to know:

Coal town Rebels- one, Allied Nazi Chickens- zero.

The Allied Japanese Tunnel Invasion

It was fall, just a few short months after the end of the Nazi Chicken Wars. Most of the rubble from the Nazi Chicken Wars had been cleared away. Unfortunately the Fortress (barn), where the last battle had been fought burned to the ground. This had to be the result of the fight with the Allied Asian Ninja's. The Coal Town Rebels were devastated, not only had they lost their beloved Fortress, all their weapons had been confiscated, pending an investigation by the Field Marshall.

The only shining light of the whole post war cleanup was the erection of the new Fortress (tin barn). The Coal Town Rebels were excited about the prospects of having a new Fortress, but they were also assigned the arduous task of resupplying the depot area (stock with new hay).

The Rebels looked forward to spring, when all restrictions would be lifted and new wars and adventures would present themselves.

It was gonna be a long winter, but there was always snow, which brought the hope of small skirmishes with the

Long Eared Assassins (rabbits) in the Coal Mine Mountains.

Spring finally came, but with spring came time to clean the Fortress, all winter rubbish from the Ogres (cows) had to be removed. The task consisted of shoveling all the rubbish into the one wheel excavation truck (wheel barrow) and transport to the landfill area (garden). The Rebels were feeling pretty good; all their weapons had been released from the armory. New recruits, Private Jack and Private Pig had arrived and were beginning their basic training. During the spring cleaning of the Fortress Lt. Dan found evidence of a possible invasion. He sent Sergeant Ray and Corporal Ben in to investigate. After carefully moving aside rubble, there it was; a tunnel!

The Coal Town Rebels leapt into action. The all troops to arms alarm was sounded (whistle), the Rebels had been under surveillance by an unknown enemy. After removal of the entire haystack the Rebels had uncovered numerous tunnels and what appeared to be enemy bedding areas. They had encountered similar enemies but not this big and not of this magnitude. This was obviously a mass invasion and had to be dealt with swiftly. Suddenly the enemy showed themselves, the Rebels were surrounded.

They pulled their weapons and began fighting the enemy; their efforts were futile.

They found their weapons to be ineffective with this new enemy. The Tunnel Infiltrators (rats) facing the Rebels had been well trained. The Tunnel Rats were fast, kept low to the ground and had protruding marble eyes. The enemy had obviously gone under some sort of transformation surgery to make their eyes more adaptable to darkness. They could have been genetically altered and bred for tunnel type invasions. The Rebels knew they had to retreat and develop new weapons and tactics before facing the Infiltrators.

Lt. Dan said he thought these enemies were Japanese; the Rebels started researching the military confidential documents (world book encyclopedia) to find the information.

Corporal Ben found something interesting; the Japanese flag looked just like the eyes of the infiltrators when a light was shown into their eyes. This confirmed Lt. Dan's suspicions, the Rebels were facing Japanese, whom were known for tunnel type invasions. Now it was time to develop effective weapons to fight this new enemy. The Tunnel Rats stayed low to the ground, so weapons would have to be developed that would be effective at low altitudes. Lt. Dan started drawing a sketch of his new prototype weapon; it would be a hand held model. Shortly after drafting the print of the new prototype weapon the Rebels assembled the necessary parts. They had it, the new "High Energy Low Altitude Slammer" (shovel).

It was time; the Rebels were prepared to assault the Infiltrators at dawn. Lt. Dan called all the troops together, they were ready, adrenaline was pumping. Then Lt. Dan yelled, "Charge".

The Rebels shot to their feet and the war was on, Private Pig was first into the Fortress, then Private Jack. As Corporal Ben burst through the entry of the Fortress, Private Pig shot back out. An Infiltrator had run up his leg and was inside his pants, this was a counter-attack the Rebels were not prepared to endure.

Retreat was sounded, the Rebels fell back, now it was obvious; they needed new armor accessories. Nobody can tolerate a rat in their drawers. When a rat starts climbing, in them pants, ya gotta come out. They went back to the drawing board; Private Jack came up with an "Anti-Infiltrator Compression Cuff" (rubber band) that could be placed on the armor to prevent entry.

The Rebels had lost the element of surprise, but they were angry and fully prepared for war. Lt. Dan yelled "charge" and they were off, rushing into the enemy. The "High Energy Low Altitude Slammer" was very effective. The Japanese Infiltrators were defeated; survivors dove back into their tunnels and left the Fortress. Lt Dan presented Private Jack and Private Pig with medals of bravery (Cracker Jack ring).

That was that, the Coal Town Rebels were back, it was time to clear the battlefield and prepare for the next excursion.

The Ogre Prisoner Transfer

It was summer; the Coal Town Rebels had just finished the aftermath cleanup of the Japanese Tunnel Invasion. The Field Marshall called the Rebels in; she had just acquired an 80-acre compound (leased pasture) to house the Ogre prisoners (cows). She had requisitioned a transport convoy (cattle truck) to deliver the Ogre prisoners to the new compound. The Coal Town Rebels were to escort the convoy; Lt. Dan knew this wasn't gonna be an easy task. These Ogre transports never went smoothly, Ogre's are nasty and mean.

Ogres will disperse green sludge onto their tails and use this toxic excrement as a weapon.

Some carry a pair of swords (horns) mounted on their head, just for skewering unwary opponents. Ogres are also skilled in the art of karate kicking; chomping, and foot stomping. They developed the now infamous head butt.

Ogres are formidable opponents skilled in the art of warfare; very large creatures that can crush a Rebel with very little effort. The expectation was to move the Ogres into a confinement chamber (corral), and then individually into the transporter.

Lt. Dan caught the first unexpected blow, karate kick to the kneecap. The cry went out "Medic" Corporal Ben rushed in to assist, before he could get to Lt. Dan, he caught the dreaded toxin coated tail. The tail wrapped around his face leaving behind the green poison that would surely kill him. The poison was in his eyes, across his lips, and dripped from the horizontal lines left on his face from the toxin. The stench alone would surely kill Corporal Ben, let alone the horrendous foul taste. He was blinded, staggering and trying to get to safety.

Private Pig ran in and assisted Lt. Dan to safety behind the cross bar force field (gate). Private Jack came to the aid of Corporal Ben; there was only one thing that would save him at this point. Corporal Ben had to be immersed into the decontamination chamber (water trough). Private Jack left Corporal Ben by the decontamination chamber, and headed to the confinement chamber. The transporter technician had managed to get the first Ogre into the transporter.

This Ogre was creating chaos by trying to break back out of the transporter; all the other Ogres were watching and acting crazy. That is one of the diversions Ogre's use to gain an upper hand during a confrontation.

The Rebels knew they were very close to having a prison riot on their hands. Private Jack jumped into the confinement chamber trying to bring the prisoners back under control.

Jack was making progress until "crunch" an Ogre had stomped on his foot. Private Jack was in intense pain, he pushed, kicked and punched the Ogre, but this Ogre was not affected. The Ogre knew he had Private Jack, right where he wanted him.

Lt. Dan jabbed the Ogre from behind with his "Hyper-Thrust Forward Motion Lance" (stick) the end of the "Hyper-Lance" made contact with the Ogre, the end disappeared for a second. The Ogre all but Jumped into the transporter. The Rebels weren't sure why that Ogre took off so quickly, that lance must have scared it. Now it was obvious this one was the ring leader of the chaotic episode. The remaining Ogres wanted no part of that lance; instead they climbed right into the transporter following the ring leader.

Returning back to the Fortress after the transport, the Coal Town Rebels couldn't believe what they saw, "Chickens". The Field Marshall had allowed new chicken recruits into the Rebels Fortress. This was unacceptable; the Rebels would have to regain their Fortress.

These chickens were small, but it was certain they would grow; there will be a new "Chicken Commander". This is the way it always starts. From the beginning, way back when General Lee and Colonel Jim fought the "Roman Chicken War", "Conquistador Chicken War", "British Chicken War" and the "French Chicken War".

New Chicken recruits were always brought in and it was not long before they took over the Fortress. Lt Dan, Corporal Ben and Sergeant Ray were enlisted and fought in the "Apache Chicken War", "Comanche Chicken War", and the "Civil Chicken War".

Once again war was imminent, against a new enemy unlike any fought before.

The Search for Mike

Weeks Later the Field Marshall finally sent down the order to sacrifice two prisoners. The Rebels knew war was close at hand; they brought the bodies to the Field Marshall and asked why she dunked them in boiling water before stripping their feathers. She said it was to loosen the feathers and get the mites off their butts. Corporal Ben asked, "Who is Mike and what's he doing on a chickens ass". Ben learned that lye soap tastes almost as bad as Ogre sludge. Due to the mouth washing the Rebels never got a clear answer of who Mike was.

The Rebels were curious now, they had to find Mike and learn why he liked chicken butts. The Rebels decided they would try to force Mike out, they would rub the chicken's butts with a corncob; that will bring him out. After about fifty chickens, the Rebels decided to try something different. Lt. Dan had a chicken upside down and told Corporal Ben to take a close look to see if Mike was anywhere near. Corporal Ben leaned way over, looking closely; Lt. Dan thrust the chicken upwards.

That was it; Ogre sludge, lye soap and now Corporal Ben had officially kissed the butt of his mortal enemy, a chicken. Corporal Ben asked; why did you, do that! Lt. Dan said he wanted to see if lye soap would flush Mike out. Corporal Ben asked, "Why didn't you just get a bar of lye soap"? Lt. Dan said he didn't think of that, and then sent Private Pig to get a bar.

Corporal Ben didn't believe Lt. Dan; on occasion he would test the grit of his troops. These tests always left a fowl taste in Corporal Ben's mouth. The Rebels rubbed lye soap on another fifty chicken butts, but no sign of Mike, they decided to call it a day and try a new plan in the morning.

Morning came; Lt. Dan had a plan, left over firecrackers from the Fourth of July. The Rebels would blast Mike out, surely this would be an effective way, to make Mike bail out! They decided to us Ladyfinger firecrackers. Private Jack caught a chicken, Lt. Dan inserted the Ladyfinger and lit it, and the chicken took off. Pop! Feathers flew, but nothing came out of the chicken. This continued the rest of the day, but no sign of Mike.

Next morning, the Field Marshall said, "what's going on with all those bare ass chickens"? Corporal Ben was wondering how he could get "her" to taste that lye soap. She told the Rebels to take a small can of kerosene and a paintbrush and dab those chickens on the butt, they obviously had something wrong with them.

The Rebels started catching chickens and slapping the kerosene on their butts with the paintbrush. The chickens would run away with their wings straight up, like a referee that had just witnessed a perfect field goal.

The Rebels weren't sure if it was the corncob rash, the lye soap rash or the powder burns that caused the kerosene to be so effective.

It was time to call off the search; they were never gonna find Mike. The vow was made to search for him during the fall butcher. Maybe he will be easier to find when the chickens are totally naked, or he might be in that pot of boiling water. The Coal Town Rebels knew they were wasting time; they had to learn more about this new battalion they were certain to fight.

The Field Marshall called the Rebels in, she told them the neighbors had a new chicken house and needed their help.

They weren't happy about leaving their fortress to help someone else secure another fortress.

After all if you have a fortress, it is your responsibility to keep it secure. When they arrived, they were escorted to the holding area. It was a virtual chicken prison, rows and rows of cells with three chickens per cell. There were several escapees that were trying to exit the compound. It would be the job of the Rebels to capture the escapees and return them to their cells. They were successful with the capture and returned the prisoners to their cells, then left the compound.

They noticed Mike had obviously been inside that compound; every chicken in there had a bare butt. So how did these people find out about Mike? Were they trying to blast him out? The Rebels must have been on the right track and these people must have been watching to find the best method to force Mike out into the open. This made them wonder, how many ladyfinger firecrackers did these people use?

There were thousands of chickens in there; they must buy firecrackers by the truckload. Mike had to be one tough commando; he must have been assigned to a covert operation. That was probably why the Field Marshall never gave a clear answer about who Mike was. The Coal Town Rebels may never meet Mike, but they were glad he was on their side. With these chickens growing faster, it would not be long before everything started falling apart.

A New Chicken Commander

The Field Marshall sent down the order, there were too many of them "Rubber Finger Head Chickens". The Field Marshall told the Rebels to sacrifice all but one, of her choosing. They finally caught and decapitated all the chosen enemies. The next morning it was obvious, the remaining rubber finger head had taken the position of Chicken Commander. This new Commander was mean; he would jump on the back of one of his own unwary troops and start pounding em in the back of the head. Lt. Dan understood discipline within the ranks, but this Commander seemed to enjoy; just being mean. After pounding one of his recruits he would jump off and stick out his chest like a Sheriff with a shiny new badge. It was obvious to the Rebels; they needed to give this Commander some of his own medicine. They had a plan. Now they had to execute the plan! And not execute the Chicken Commander. After all they wanted to teach it a lesson, and not be taught one themselves! The Field Marshall had picked that Commander and if they went too far they knew the lye soap incident would be minor in comparison to what they would get.

The Rebels decided to sneak up on "Ole Rubber Finger Head". They started sneaking through the tall grass; Lt. Dan punched Corporal Ben in the ribs and pointed ahead. There he was, whipping the fire out of one of his troops. They moved forward, the Chicken Commander had his back to them.

Lt. Dan yelled "Now". They jumped and caught the Rubber Finger Head, now to install the brain clamps. (Spring clothes pins). The Rebels installed two brain clamps on the rubber fingers and turned the Chicken Commander loose.

The Commander flopped his head to the side and the clamp slapped him in the face, he threw his head the other way and got slapped by the other clamp. This was a good plan, that Ole Rubber Finger head was flogging himself. The Rebels were admiring their work when a broom hit Lt. Dan in the back of the head. "Oh Fudge" the Field Marshall had caught em red handed. Corporal Ben said, "It ain't no big deal", "Just a training session". "You get those things off that Chicken or there is going to be more than one training session". The Field Marshall sure took things serious. They took off to catch the rubber finger head and get the brain clamps off.

The Rebels needed to regain some of their fortress. The first thing to do was build an enemy barricade to push the enemy back. Once built the barricade was put in place. Made of horizontal rails and vertical slats, this should work. The only thing on the other side of the barricade was an old grease gun and the chickens couldn't use that against em. The next morning the Rebels checked the barricade to make sure it was working." Spies", those chickens were sticking their heads through the slats and spying on em. The Rebels decided to make a weapon to counteract this behavior, Private Pig had an idea.

They went to work making the new weapon, "Double Slug Spy Buster" (gunny sack with corn in it). It was time to test the weapon; Private Jack crawled along the panel until he got close to a spy. The spy stuck his head out and "whack"; the thrust knocked the spy backwards onto his back. The spy was stunned, he was on his back, legs kicking like he was riding a bicycle upside down. Several more "Double Slug Spy Busters" were made.

The Rebels continued for several hours, busting spies and watching em pedal. Once in a while Lt. Dan would grab the head of a spy and pull.

The chicken's neck would stretch way out, and it would make an "EERRKK" noise like tires on pavement. He decided to quit doing that because the chickens were leaving feathers behind, when he let go and their head snapped back. The stretchy chickens would fall back' but only on their butts, like they were waiting for the head to catch up with the body.

The Chicken Commander started jumping on his disabled spies and pounding em as soon as they could roll back over on their bellies.

What an evil leader, the war coming up was not gonna be easy; his troops were gonna be tough. Corporal Ben sure wanted to give him another taste of those brain clamps. This Commander wasn't anything like the Nazi Commander the Rebels had fought before. This Commander was shorter and darker in color.

Lt. Dan said he had been investigating and was pretty darn sure, this chump was Korean.

Korean or not, with him pounding those troops every day, it was not gonna be an easy war. The Rebels knew they were gonna have to build better weapons.

They started drawing blue prints of the new weapons needed to defeat the Korean Chickens. Corporal Ben had a new device. Lt. Dan was very interested. Ben had developed a "Long Range Sonic Boom Rifle" (cap gun with 4 foot long ½ copper pipe taped to the end). Lt. Dan wanted to test this thing out; the Rebels started crawling in the tall grass. Chicken up ahead, the Korean chump had just got finished pounding, and it was still laying on its belly. Lt. Dan slid the rifle toward the chicken. He had it positioned right behind the eye, where a chicken hides their ear. "Pow", that chickens head snapped over to the other side. It popped up and started running in a circle, squawking like crazy.

This may not have been a good idea; the whole chicken army was beating down upon the Rebels, and that Korean Commander was in the lead. Corporal Ben jumped up and started running, the other Rebels followed. Lt. Dan asked Corporal Ben "why did you run"?

Ben said "there is no way I was gonna lay there and let that Korean Chump jump on my back". You've seen what he does to his own troops. What do you think he would do to us?

The Korean Chicken Commander was mad; the Rebels had wounded one of his troops. They knew that he wanted revenge. Well back to work, the Rebels would keep the "Long Range Sonic Boom Rifle"; it was good for creating distractions. Private Jack had a new weapon that looked promising; it was a "Double Back Chicken Lure" (plastic worm on a string).

Time for a test, Jack threw the lure by two chickens that had their backs turned toward the Rebels. Jack started pulling; the chickens doubled back and took off trying to catch the lure. The chickens ran right up to them, where they got a serious whack with a corncob, of course they started flopping' and squawking. "Old Lord" here come the whole chicken army again. The Rebels took off and found another place to build weapons. Private Pig had developed an "Aerial Chicken Smoke Bomb" (news paper full of dirt rolled into a ball).

The Rebels launched a couple of the smoke bombs, the bombs hit the ground and "poof" big dust cloud, and the chickens went crazy. They took off running, colliding with each other, running into the fence, and slapping each other. This was a keeper! Sergeant Ray built an "Anti-Chicken Shrapnel Bomb" (gravel wrapped in plastic wrap). Time for a test, Ray launched the shrapnel bomb.

The bomb hit the ground flew apart and the gravel pelted the chickens; they were staggering backwards with their wings out to the side. Lt. Dan said see how stupid they are? Why didn't they cover their heads with their wings? Lt. Dan said "we will keep it". Lt. Dan's weapon was a "Close Range Chicken Slinger" (wire with a hook bent on one end). The Rebels slipped down by the chickens. Lt. Dan slid the slinger over by a chicken and then jerked. The slinger caught the foot of the chicken; the chicken had a surprised, dumb look on his face as he went by over the Rebels heads. Its eyes seemed to be wider than usual and its beak was open, tongue stuck out, but it never squawked a sound. The chicken was slung about ten feet away. It was a keeper!

With the new arsenal, the Rebels were prepared for war. They sat back anticipating the call from the Field Marshall.

The Korean Chicken War

The call finally came; it was time to assault the "Korean Chickens". Lt. Dan called the Rebels together; he said the Field Marshall wanted the Korean Chicken Commander and twenty of his soldiers taken alive. That "stinks" the Rebels shouted, "Are we gonna have to put up with this Commander forever"? Lt. Dan said "all I know is she wants him alive"! Corporal Ben thought to himself, "well maybe for now". Dan said; she wanted to know about them pullets with feathers missing on their neck. Do you think she knew I was pulling on them chickens? The Rebels said in unison "No Way" she wasn't around. Lt. Dan asked; well why do ya figure she called em pullets, if she didn't know I was pullin' em? Jack said; I bet she seen that Ole Commander on top of one em and thought he was tryin' to pull it through the yard. They all agreed, that had to be it, heck that Ole Commander was always jumpin' on one of his troops.

Lt. Dan said "it is time to go boys" then he yelled "CHARGE". The Rebels were off; they were headed for the door of the Fortress.

All of a sudden they were being driven back, how did those chickens know they was comin'? Then the 1st Mechanized Artillery Squad came busting out of the Fortress. They had decided to attack from the rear, which put the Rebels right in the line of fire.

 Lt. Dan called "retreat"; he then scolded the 1st Mechanized Artillery Squad for putting the Rebels in harm's way. All attacks were to be coordinated through him. Corporal Ben said "Blah Blah Blah"; let's get on with it. Lt. Dan didn't like mealy mouth talk; he said keep it up and you will sit this one out.

Corporal Ben wanted to thump that Commander bad, so he decided to just shut up. He would hit Lt. Dan with one of them "Aerial Chicken Smoke Bombs" when he wasn't lookin'!

All right no more mistakes, full frontal attack; Lt. Dan yelled "CHARGE" and the Rebels were off again. They burst through the door of the Fortress and were met by a squad of Korean Taekwondo Chickens. These Taekwondo chickens weren't slapping like regular chickens, they would jump up and sling their claws, then come down with a wing on edge like a knife.

The Rebels fell back; it was time for a diversion. Corporal Ben was sent in with the "Long Range Sonic Boom Rifle", he was to pop the ear of a Taekwondo chicken and hopefully they would Taekwondo each other. Corporal Ben crawled inside the door of the Fortress.

There they were all gathered up pecking at crickets. Corporal Ben slid the rifle forward, raised it up next to the chickens ear, "Pop". Oh no! The chicken had turned around just as Ben pulled the trigger.

The Taekwondo chicken clamped its eyes shut and fell over on its side, the chicken started trying to run but it was still on its side and was only spinning in a circle.

Corporal Ben looked up and the rest of those Taekwondo chickens were on him.

Corporal Ben started crawling backward trying to get out the door. "Boom" he felt something splatter all over him, he started looking to see if he was bleeding, no blood! Just a big dirt cloud. Private Pig had sent in an "Aerial Chicken Smoke Bomb". The Taekwondo chickens backed away and started running in the confusion. Ben backed out the door then ran back to the squad.

First aid was rendered to get the dirt out of Ben's ears; Lt. Dan said all right let's go. The Rebels were off; Lt. Dan said, "Let's get behind that barricade we made". They leapt behind the barricade where the chicken spies hung out. Oh Crud! The Korean Chicken Commander was in there pounding one of his troops. The Chicken Commander was surprised but he only hesitated a second before jumping at the Rebels. The Chicken Commander was flying through the air with his talons aimed right at Private Jack.

"Oh Lord" that crazy chicken was squirting divinity at them. All of a sudden the Chicken Commander went straight up; he looked like he was riding a rainbow!

The Chicken Commander landed at the Fortress door and ran out. At the last second Lt. Dan had swung the "Close Range Chicken Slinger" and caught the foot of that Korean chump. Jack said "thanks", Lt. Dan said don't thank me yet we still have a big battle ahead.

The Rebels were inside the Fortress, but now those chickens were between them and the door, the Rebels were cornered. They thought about bolting for the door, but the Taekwondo chickens had already blocked the doorway. It was gonna be a fight to the death, the Rebels needed a plan. All of a sudden the wind blew hard and the door slammed shut.

They were really trapped now; even if they got past the Taekwondo chickens, they would have to slow down to open the door. The Chickens were advancing, Private Pig grabbed Sergeant Ray's "Anti Chicken Shrapnel Bomb", tossed it at the chickens, and the chickens were pelted by the gravel, they fell back. Private Jack flipped the Double Back Chicken lure out and started pulling. Every time he flipped it out a chicken would chase it back and Jack would thump it with a corncob.

Sergeant Ray had caught the chicken that the Korean Commander had been pounding; maybe the Rebels can use this chicken against the others. Lt. Dan said "hurry, see if we can find a cricket".

They would use grease from the old grease gun to stick the cricket to the chickens head. There was no way the chicken could see it, but the others would. Private Pig caught the cricket; the Rebels were in business again. The Rebels stuck the cricket to the chicken's head and turned it loose on the other side of the barricade. The Taekwondo chickens saw the cricket and went after it; they were chasing the cricket chicken all over the Fortress.

The Rebels had an opportunity and they were gonna take advantage. All of a sudden Lt. Dan was hit in the back of the head with an "Aerial Chicken Smoke Bomb"; Corporal Ben said sorry, I was tryin' to confuse em and didn't know you were in the way. The Rebels jumped over the barricade and attacked. They were gaining ground; Lt. Dan shouted remember twenty chicken troops and the Chicken Commander have to be taken alive. The Rebels started catching the chicken troops and stuffing them into the small chicken pen.

There weren't many chicken troops left and they had not seen the Chicken Commander. Finally Private Jack yelled; there he is, let's get him. They took off; he had been hiding in the tall grass by the landfill area.

The Rebels finally captured the Korean Chicken Commander. He started throwing his head around like he knew those brain clamps were coming. Before stuffing him in the pen, Corporal Ben sucker punched him twice. The field Marshall came over and said I told you twenty chicken troops and there are only nineteen in that pen. Oh Man! The Rebels had made a mistake. Hold on! A noise in the grass, they went to investigate, right there, the cricket chicken. The cricket had slid down and the chicken was trying to eat it. Another campaign had gone in their favor; the Rebels were feeling good about everything. Except that Korean Chicken Commander, but Corporal Ben had plans for him.

Someday when least expected that Commander was gonna get what he deserved! There wasn't gonna be a brain clamp involved, more like a brain buster.

The Dark Screaming Zombie

Shortly after the Korean Chicken War, the Rebels were out after dark finishing chores they had put off. A long eared assassin had ventured into their territory; it had to be chased away, and they lost track of time. Through the dark they heard a scream; the Rebels ran and hid behind the decontamination chamber. They could see a figure walking strangely through the field. This thing looked like a man, but it was walking like the left leg was stiff, out to the side. Lt. Dan said I think it's a "Zombie" that got killed ridin' a scooter. Look how he uses his left leg, out to the side like he is pushing hisself along. The Rebels continued to watch the Zombie. When it got to the cross fence, he made several attempts to climb over. He got straddle of the fence and was hopping up and down and screaming. Chills ran up the spines of the Rebels, just then the Field Marshall yelled, "What are you doing out there? "Get in here".

The Rebels jumped up and ran into headquarters; they had to defend the compound against the Zombie.

Lt. Dan called the troops together; we will watch to see if he comes back tomorrow. The next day the Rebels were busy, they wanted all their duties to be done so they could focus on the Zombie. Nightfall came, the Rebels waited and waited but no Zombie. Maybe the Zombie had found what it was looking for. The Field Marshall called them in for the evening.

The Rebels were anxious; they had all kinds of questions in their minds. They were gonna find the answers, even if it meant they would become Zombies to. Corporal Ben was suddenly awakened, Lt. Dan was shaking him. "Do you hear that"? The Zombie was back!

The Rebels slipped down the stairs and out of headquarters. They crawled behind the decontamination chamber and looked across the field. There it was, let's slip down closer, Lt. Dan said. The Rebels started crawling on their bellies, toward the Zombie. Suddenly the Zombie stopped, the Rebels tried to hide as best they could in the weeds. The Zombie started wrestling with his ragged clothes, "Old Lord" what is he doin' asked Corporal Ben? Lt. Dan poked him in the ribs. "Oh Crud" the Zombie looked in their direction.

The Rebels lay still, it seemed like forever. They just knew that Zombie was looking at them. "He's sprayin' Zombie poison on the grass" Lt. Dan whispered. The Zombie wrestled with his clothes again and then made a noise like a "deep in the cave growl". The Zombie cast a stare in the Rebels direction, "Oh No" he's gonna come over here and spray us with Zombie poison, Ben said. Lt. Dan poked him in the ribs again. Then they smelled it! That Zombie had let off toxic death gas. That must have been the "deep in the cave growl". Lt. Dan whispered, "Whew that Zombie is definitely dead! Cover you face with your nightshirt and try not to breathe.

The Zombie started walking sideways again. The Rebels stayed where they were, they had gotten close enough. If you smell Zombie poison death gas you're too close. The Zombie got to the cross fence and started hopping and screaming. He fell over the fence and rolled around on the ground. "What's he doin' Corporal Ben asked"? Lt. Dan said I think he's diggin' up grubs and eatin' em, can't you hear him growlin'. "You know Zombies are full of worms". The Zombie finally stood up and staggered into the old shack of a house.

The Rebels saw the light come on at headquarters; Lt. Dan said, "Darn we're busted. The Rebels ran back to headquarters, the light went off, o.k. they can slip in and the Field Marshall will never know they were gone. The Rebels crept toward the stairs being careful not to make any noise. Suddenly the light came on. The Field Marshall yelled what is that smell? The Rebels looked down; they were covered in Ogre sludge from crawling in the field. The Field Marshall made them strip out of their nightclothes and bathe. She never said much but the Rebels knew, there would be double work tomorrow. The Field Marshall decided the Rebels had too much energy; they could pull weeds from the landfill (garden). They weren't happy, weed the whole landfill on top of their other duties! Well maybe, it was worth it to learn more about that Zombie. Lt. Dan whistled, the other Rebels looked up, Dan pointed toward the old shack. That old man Gabe came walking out of the shack.

Was the Zombie living in that house with "Ole Gabe"? Maybe the Zombie is Gabe's brother? Maybe Gabe is the Zombie at night.

This called for some more investigation; the Rebels were gonna sneak out again. That night the Field Marshall said "you numbskulls better stay in your beds tonight". You know there are bad things out there that will eat you. They knew she was talking about the Zombie; she must have seen it herself and was trying to protect them. Everybody knows Zombies are brain suckers. There was no way; they could be Rebels without a brain. Who would wipe the drool off their faces? Nobody wanted to do that and fight chickens at the same time. No! Without a brain, a Rebel would be just about worthless. Well, maybe they could be used to test chicken fighting weapons on. No matter!

The Rebels were gonna find out about this Zombie, if it cost a brain or two, then so be it!

The Rebels decided they needed helmets that would at least slow the brain sucking down, off to the armory (back porch). They looked around, moving things, and then private Pig said "up there". There they were, "helmets" (gallon lard buckets) they were up on the shelf. It took a little while to get them down without the Field Marshall catching them.

They stayed awake planning their next move, as soon as the Field Marshall fell asleep; they were gonna be on the Zombies trail. The Rebels slipped down the stairs and out the door. They decided to back track the Zombie; he came from the same direction every night. He might be sucking the brains of neighbors up the hill. The Rebels ran up the hill, snuck around some of the neighbor houses. No Zombie! Where in the world was he coming from? Sergeant Ray said look! The Rebels turned. They saw him over on another road, like he was coming from town. "Oh brother he was walking toward the road they were on. Run shouted Lt. Dan, the Rebels were off. Their helmets were banging against their ears, and the chinstrap pulling on their throats. When they got to the fence they realized the force field was still on (electric fence). Maybe the force field was causing the Zombie to spray the poison?

The Rebels climbed the walnut tree next to the fence and jumped over to the other side. Lt. Dan said follow me, we'll hide next to the "Mud Sliders Pen" (hogs). The Rebels hid. They waited quite awhile, and then Private Pig said "here he comes". The Zombie tried crawling over the fence.

He started hopping up and down and screaming, he smelled bad like somebody soaked him in booze. Lt. Dan said Zombies don't like to drink blood like Vampires. They like brains, grubs and whiskey.

The Zombie fell over, then stood and started walking again. Wait! He stopped! He started wrestling with his clothes. He is spraying poison. The force field was causing the Zombie to spray poison. Then they heard it a "deep in the cave growl". "Oh Brother" they didn't want to die from Zombie poison gas. They jumped up and started running. Lt. Dan looked back; the Zombie was waving at them. "Crud" boys we are in trouble, he waved to let us know he will be comin' for us.

The Rebels didn't wait to see if the Zombie stopped to eat grubs on the other side of the cross fence.

The next morning Lt Dan handed out "Anti-Zombie Crucifixes" (Popsicle sticks broken and glued together) to all the troops. He gave two to each of them. Lt. Dan said put one in the front of your unders and one in the back. That will keep ya' from gettin' the poison spray and the "deep in the cave growl".

Corporal Ben didn't mind the front cross, but the one in back kept slippin' tween his bubbles. It was really annoying and painful when he sat down. During lunch the Field Marshall said what is the matter with you dummies can't you sit still. Private Jack whispered "I would like to see her sit still with a stick tween her bubbles".

After lunch the Rebels went back outside. Maybe "Ole Gabe" was being held prisoner, and that Zombie was sucking on his brain a little at a time. That would explain why he never came outside much anymore. They should probably sneak down there and investigate.

Corporal Ben got a bellyache. "Oh Man" was he gettin' the "deep in the cave growl"? Ben held it as long as he could. "Oh no" here it comes. Instead of a growl, there was a loud whistle. Corporal Ben was thinkin', Lt. Dan was right, that crucifix tween his bubbles stopped the growl, and turned it into a whistle. Ben turned around and the rest of the Rebels were staring at him. Corporal Ben said "what are you guys lookin' at"? Lt Dan said, "You're the one that whistled". Corporal Ben played it off and said, "I was just goofin' around". Lt. Dan said lets sneak down and look in the shack, maybe we can see if "Ole Gabe" needs to be rescued from that Zombie. Corporal Ben saw him lean over and tell Private Pig, "Keep an eye on him". "Man" Lt. Dan thought Ben was turnin' into a Zombie.

Lt. Dan told Private Pig "That's the way it starts, after losin' some of their brain, they do stuff and don't know why. If he starts lookin' for grubs, or tries to spray the grass with poison, whack him!

The Rebels started out across the field toward "Ole Gabes"; all of a sudden they heard sirens. Coppers and an ambulance, pulled in by "Ole Gabe's". Did somebody else see that Zombie, or smell the poison gas?

They brought "Ole Gabe" out and put him in the ambulance. Lt. Dan said that Zombie musta been comin' after us and "Ole Gabe" tried to stop him. Later that day the Field Marshall told the Rebels "Ole Gabe" died. The Zombie killed our friend "Ole Gabe". They waited every night, thinking the Zombie is out there and he will be coming back. They were gonna catch that Zombie and put an end to him, for killin' their good friend. They liked "Ole Gabe" a lot, he always smiled and waved at em.

The Rebels were making plans. They had constructed "Zombie Mortifying Crucifix Daggers" (two sticks nailed together and sharpened on one end). Their plan was to have two Rebels slip in behind the Zombie and jab him with the "Crucifix Dagger" and run before he could get them with the "deep in the cave growl". The other Rebels would get him from the front when he started to turn. They knew he would have to wrestle with his clothes before he could spray poison.

That would give em time, to take him down. The Zombie never came back. The Rebels figured "Ole Gabe" musta torn him up pretty bad. Yep! That Zombie musta crawled off and double died.

After all Zombies are already dead, that's why they eat grubs. The grubs crawlin' around inside makes them feel alive. Once they double die, there ain't no brain suckin', grub eatin' or whiskey slurpin'. They're just goners.

There's always a dip in the ground where Zombies die. They dig a hole straight down and bury their self headfirst. The Rebels went down to "Ole Gabes" shack and looked around on the ground. They found it, a dip in the ground with yellow grass on top. That zombie must of sprayed poison on the ground and then dug in.

Probably had one of them "deep in the cave growls" while he was in the hole. That's what caused the hole to cave in. That Zombie ate his last grub. The Rebels saw a broken bird egg laying on the ground next to that dip. They didn't know what that was all about. Maybe that Zombie is an egg sucker to, and got one more before diggin' in. The Rebels weren't sure, but one day maybe they would find the answer. That Zombie wasn't gonna bother them no more. Anyway's that's what Lt. Dan say's and he has always been right. Well time to get those stinkin' "Anti-Zombie Crucifixes" out of their unders.

The Coal Mine Mountain Horror

After "Ole Gabe" same as killed that Zombie, the Rebels were getting bored. They moped around trying to figure out what to do, but they had not found one adventure. It was dark so they decided to catch some fireflies; they figured they could use them to make a flashlight. They would put them in a jar and then put the jar in a flour sack. When they took the sack off, it would be like turning on a flashlight. The Rebels hadn't tested it yet but they reckoned it would work.

They heard a noise; Lt. Dan said, "Be quiet". The Rebels got real still and listened, it sounded like a girl screaming. They started following the sound; it was coming from the Coal Mine Mountain. The Rebels were gonna find out what was goin' on over there. They started crawling through the fence, there it is again, must be a girl in trouble over there. Let's go boys; Lt. Dan was ready for anything. Then the Field Marshall yelled, "where are you going, get in here". Dang, we finally get an important mission and she makes us come in for the night.

When the Rebels got inside headquarters, Lt. Dan told the Field Marshall there must be a girl over there screamin'. The Field Marshall said, "She probably saw you dummies, that's enough to make any girl scream". You better stay in that bed tonight, no sneaking out, and coming back in here stinking to high heaven.

Ben thought, "Is there a "Low Heaven"? Maybe that would be their next mission, find "Low Heaven" and that Korean Chicken Commander would be a good test specimen to help find it. Lt. Dan winked at the Rebels and said let's go to bed boys.

They climbed the stairs to the barracks, they were going out tonight and they needed a plan. All right boys, Lt. Dan said we are goin' over there and see what's goin' on. The Rebels slipped down the stairs and out the door. The stars were shining and the moon was out, they didn't have time to make a flashlight, it took too long to catch all those fireflies. They decided to squeeze their eyes shut real tight and when they opened them they could see better in the dark. They were all squeezing their eyes tight and all of a sudden "Bang"! Private Pig opened his eyes and all he could see was sparkles.

The Field Marshall had whacked him in the head from behind. Get in that house and stay in there, they knew she was serious. The Rebels went back up the stairs to the barracks.

The next day they got their chores done early so they could focus on war preparations. They already had helmets from the Zombie war, now they needed to decide what weapon they would carry. They sorted through their swords, slingshots and other homemade weaponry. Then Lt. Dan looked up, there they were hanging from the rafter in the basement. The "Moon Ball Wizard Staffs".

That night after they were sent to their barracks, Lt. Dan said O.K. boy's new plan. Follow me! They slipped across the hall, through the girl's barracks and out the window. Well what now Corporal Ben asked. Follow me dummy and shut up. Man! he must think he's the Field Marshall to be talkin' like that. Down the roof onto the armory, they went, then down onto the porch. Grab your helmets and "Moon Ball Wizard Staffs" (cane pole with a glass marble jammed in the end).

The Rebels liked the staff; it could be used to knock down weeds and part blackberry briars.

It could be used as a walking staff or whacking an enemy, and the "Moon Ball" on top caught the moonlight making it easier to find a fellow Rebel in the dark.

The Rebels grabbed their helmets and staffs; down the hill and through the fence they went. They were walking cautiously across to "Camel Hump". Suddenly a scream! The Rebels took off. They were stopped instantly; somethin' had a hold of their feet. They couldn't walk, run or move. Man they were stuck in "Foot Suck Ditch" (boggy area that sucks shoes off). The Rebels finally got loose and started over "Camel Hump". Another scream, the Rebels turned and the weeds were parting like that Old Man Moses did the Red Sea. Get down shouted Lt. Dan. The Rebels kissed the dirt. What is it asked Corporal Ben? Lt. Dan said shhh! They waited, all quiet. Private Jack said I think it's gone.

The Rebels stood and looked around. No movement! Lt Dan, said let's look for tracks. The Rebels looked around, they found some scuffed up ground, but couldn't find any tracks.

They proceeded over "Camel Hump" and dropped down to the base of "Elephant Mound". Another scream coming from the left! They walked down between the base of Camel Hump and Elephant Mound. Look said Lt. Dan; the weeds were parting just like before, except this time going away from them.

Let's go! They only took a couple steps, right in front of them a Skunk. The last time they got sprayed, the Field Marshall made them bathe outside with the cold water hose. They didn't like to bathe outside naked, that cold water made em stiffin up, kinda like when the old doctor gives em a shot in their sittin' bubbles.

37

Jack threw a rock; Lt. Dan saw him and yelled no, but too late. "Poison garlic Gas", they jumped sideways and only got the tail mist. But that was enough to make them choke and gag. Nobody wants to get a direct hit from a skunk, if you do, "you die", they weren't sure how but figured you just suffocate. No! One direct hit and it's flat on the back in the ground dirt sandwich and they would be the meat.

Let's call it a night said Lt. Dan. Next morning at breakfast, the girls were all sneezing and coughing. The Field Marshall said you girls need to learn to shut that window at night. The Rebels looked at each other, and knew what each was thinking.

After Breakfast, Ben said we need to remember to close that window when we go out. Dan said let's go talk to "Ole Paulino" (Mexican Gentleman) he owns that place. I bet he has seen or heard something. Off to "Ole Paulino's" they went. They couldn't understand much of what he said, and they didn't think he understood what they said. After they left Ben asked Dan. What did that "hole o' seen oars" (hola senors) mean anyway, he said it to us when we walked up? Lt. Dan said I think it means you need to find a hole with boat oars stickin' out. Ben said, I think he's been watchin' us to, he said "seen your odd E O's" (senor adios) just before we left. What do you make of that? Lt. Dan said, I think he means he seen our odd lookin' staffs and to keep em ready.

That night, across the hall and out the window they went, making sure to close it behind them this time. They decided to drop down by "Ole Gabes" shack and then across to Gray Peak.

They came up close to Gray Peak and there was a scream.

It was close; they dropped down to their bellies and crawled through the weeds. Another scream, they crept forward, Lt. Dan asked; "what's that stink"? Corporal Ben said why do ya always ask me? I didn't do it! Lt. Dan parted the weeds, with his staff, a possum, and his head was sticking out of a dead Ogre's butt. Corporal Ben asked; do you think them Ogre's are swallowin' them possums and they're too big to push out the back end?

Lt Dan said well, that would splain the screamin', but I think we better keep lookin'. They crawled around the Ogre and down toward the base of Gray Peak. Another scream, Lt. Dan said I think it's comin' from down there. See that old mine hole with the boards stickin' out? Yep, that "Ole Paulino" knew what he was talkin' about, "hole o' seen oars".

 Let's go! They jumped up and ran behind a tree close to the hole. Another scream and it was coming from inside that hole. Lt. Dan said let's clear that hole out, so's we can see in there better. They started digging with their bare hands, pulling dirt and old boards out of the hole.

They had it widened out enough they could slide in on their bellies to see what was in there. Who's goin' in? asked Lt. Dan. Nobody volunteered, o.k. let's draw straws. Corporal Ben got the short straw; Lt. Dan said we will tie this rope around you.

If somethin' happens, just yell and we'll pull you out.

Ben didn't like this plan, but it was his duty. He lay down and started crawling into the hole. He had his staff and was poking out ahead. He felt his staff hit something mushy. He moved his arm around and pulled his helmet back where he could see better. Still can't see, he took the helmet off and tossed it behind him.

Then he saw eyes lookin' at him, what in the world is that. He lay there trying to get his eyes adjusted so he could see better.

Still couldn't see, well maybe he could poke with his staff again. All of a sudden a scream and somethin' lit on his head.

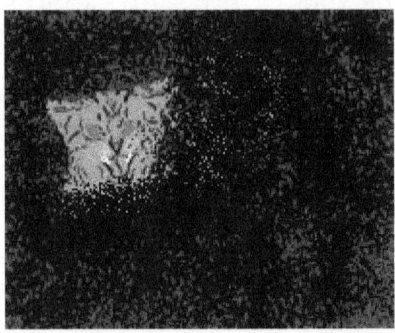

Ben yelled; Pull! Pull! Pull! Nothin' happened. Whatever this thing was it was diggin' his brains out. Maybe that Zombie had pups. They are probably brain suckers to. He yelled again; Pull! Pull! Pull! still nothin'. He was tryin' to back up but that helmet was caught between his feet. Dang will you please "Pull", this things killin' me! Then, he saw more eyes and they were movin' toward him. Whatever it was it was hissin'. He came down with his staff and pinned whatever it was to the ground. It was havin' a squallin' fit. Meantime he was tryin' to protect his brain from that diggin' Hisser on his head. Pull! Pull! then something grabbed his ankle and was pulling him out. His head hit the top of the hole and drug that brain diggin hisser off. It was Lt. Dan pullin him out! Man where were you guys? Whatever is in there was tryin' to eat me alive. The rope was snagged on an old board said Lt. Dan, that's why I came in and drug you out.

What was it anyway? Corporal Ben said; there's more than one and I don't know what it is.

"Ole Paulino" was right; I don't care if that staff does look odd, I would'a been a cooked chicken without it. I had one tryin' to get my brain out, and another one comin' in to help it. If I didn't have that staff, I would'a lost my brain for sure. Well we better get back to headquarters; we will come up with a better plan tomorrow.

The next morning at breakfast, the Field Marshall asked Ben "what in the world happened to the hair on the back of your head"? Lt. Dan said he got gum in it and we had to cut it out. Looks like you might've got carried away, what are all those cuts and scratches? Dan said, well I'm not a very good barber. The Field Marshall poked Ben with her finger right on that sore spot and said, "Don't be letting that dummy whack on that hair. Next thing you know he will be trying to take that marble brain of yours out. Whew, if she only knew how close he came to losin' that brain last night. Well, they got outta that mess, Lt. Dan said let's go boy's.

The rebels wanted to get all of their duties out of the way; they were going out again tonight. They knew where to go, but needed a new plan. Lt. Dan said I'm workin' on somethin' that should bring that "screamin' hisser" out of that hole.

That night they made it out the window without being detected, the moon was dark and it was foggy. Lt. Dan said we are gonna bring that critter out of there with a flame thrower.

They got to the hole and Lt. Dan said gather around boys, catch anything that comes out, and don't let go! He lit the flame thrower and tossed it back in the hole. There a scream, now a squall. Here they come boys.

The first "Screamin Hisser" lit on Corporal Ben. Ben said "what do you mean catch it, get the dang thing off of me! He had both hands on his helmet. His brain was already sore and he wasn't givin' this thing another shot at it. Then they were all covered, they were fighting, whatever it was, it was mean. Then another burst out of the hole and it was dragging fire with it. It was so foggy they couldn't see what it was but it was furry. Private Jack got his critter off and helped Private Pig get his off. Then both started pulling the critters off Sergeant Ray, Lt. Dan and Corporal Ben. I can't hold on to em said Jack they bite and claw too much, and it's too dark and foggy to tell what they are. The critters were finally all gone, but that one dragging the fire had set the grass on fire. Lt. Dan said boys we better get that fire put out or we are gonna be suspended again. The Rebels stomped the fire out and used their helmets to dump water on the ground from the ditch behind the tree.

Lt. Dan looked the Rebels over. They had scratches all over, take your helmets boys and fill em up with blackberries. Blackberries! What in the world do we need blackberries for? Lt. Dan said the only way to splain all them scratches to the Field Marshall is blackberry briars.

They filled their helmets with berries, and headed for headquarters. The Field Marshall met them at the door; she was going to tell them it was time for breakfast. The Field Marshall asked why they were all scratched up. Lt. Dan said "we decided to pick berries this mornin'". The Field Marshall, said well go eat breakfast and I'll make a cobbler with these berries. The Rebels never heard another scream from the Coal Mine Mountains.

Another enemy defeated, they just didn't know what the enemy was, other than a "screamin' hisser".

Finding Low Heaven

There weren't any missions in sight, so the Rebels decided to answer that question about "Low Heaven". It just made sense, if there's a "High Heaven", there has to be a "Low Heaven". They were sure there's a High Heaven cause the Field Marshall always mentioned it. This mission shouldn't take very long, it's not like they would be tracking and fighting an enemy. They would have to use their brains and figure it out. They knew high heaven was to far up to reach. Some say, one of them priests or preachers has to throw "Holy Water" on you. And then you had to be "Bath Tized", they didn't like that idea. The last time they saw that happen to a fella in church, that "Ole Preacher" same as drowned him. They didn't mind the Bath part, but that Tized looked dangerous. They figured that's the part where the "Ole Preacher" dunks somebody under and starts talkin' till they're drowned and then drags em out of that tank. Then they wrap a towel around him and say a bunch of words. Then everybody gathers around and starts pumpin' his arms and slappin' his back to get the water knocked back out of him so he's undrowned.

That's takin' things too serious and goin too far! Drowned and undrowned just looks too painful. But they shouldn't have to do that to find low heaven.

Lt. Dan, Sergeant Ray and Corporal Ben agreed, if somebody had to be "Bath Tized" then one of them Privates would be picked. Just to give em the opportunity to move up in rank.

The first thing to do was go to Gray Peak. They would stand on top and look up to see if they could find low heaven. Maybe there's a line or mark of some kind that separates Low Heaven from High Heaven.

They looked and looked, but all they saw was spots. Next they would throw rocks up in the air, if they got hung and didn't come back down, then that's where Low Heaven started. They threw a dozen rocks each but they all came back down. Well back to the Fortress, they saw spots the rest of the day. That obviously wasn't going to be the way to find low heaven. The next morning Corporal Ben said, well let's get that "Ole Korean Commander" and toss him in the air. If he finds low heaven he will stay up there, if not he will come back down. They caught the Ole Commander and tossed him in the air. He looked happy, so maybe he got close.

Well not close enough, here he comes back down. Lt. Dan said well maybe we need to be higher up. Let's get on the roof of the armory and toss him up. Lt. Dan got up and Corporal Ben handed him the Ole Commander. Up he went, he looked even happier than last time. Oh crud, here he comes back down. When Ole Commander hit the ground he sounded like a Zombie growl may have come out of him. Well the Fortress is next highest said Sergeant Ray.

They got the ladder out and propped it against the Fortress. Ben went up and Lt. Dan handed him Ole Commander. Ben threw him up into the air, he looked even happier. Man here he comes back down. Make sure you get him after he hits the ground, yelled Corporal Ben. The Ole Commander tried to glide in for a landing; he was coming in at an angle but going way to fast to make a smooth landing. The "Ole Korean Commander" ended up rolled in a ball. He got up and was staggering around. When the Rebels started chasing him to get him ready for his next test he took off running sideways. The Rebels finally caught him.

Well Gray Peak was next highest.

The Rebels finally climbed to the top of Gray Peak and made their way to the and made their way to the southeast end. There was a shear drop off from that end. Lt. Dan handed Ole Commander over. Corporal Ben tossed the Ole Commander up and he really looked happy. Oh Brother he's comin' back down fast, they watched as he hit the ground. He had glided in, but same problem, he was going too fast and tumbled around before stopping. He then rolled over on his belly and just laid there, like he was ready for the next flight. Let's go get him Lt. Dan said. They had to go back to the other end of Gray Peak and then drop down to the base. Then they had to follow the ravine to the spot where Ole Commander landed. He was gone; they looked around but never found him. Maybe his soul stayed in Low heaven and all that came back was bones and feathers. But where did the bones and feathers go?

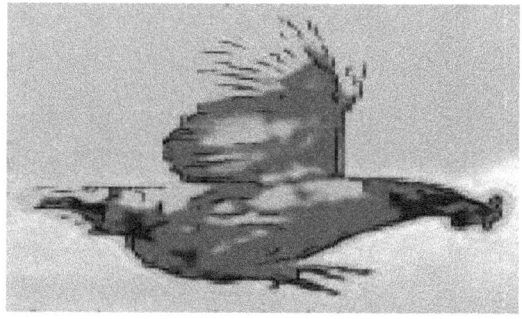

They heard the Field Marshall yelling for them, so they hoofed it back to headquarters. They had to go to the cemetery to pay their respects to the old deads that was pushin' up daisies. They helped put fresh flowers on the graves and pull weeds from around the headstones. Lt. Dan poked Ben in the ribs and pointed. There was a bird nest right on the ground, with eggs in it. That's interestin'!

What do bird nests and deads pushin' up daisies have in common? And why were those eggs right on the ground in the cemetery? They finally figured, those birds might be eatin the daisies. So if the old deads are pushin' the daisies up, what's keepin' the daisies out of the nest? The Rebels looked that nest over pretty good. Then they saw it, a broken egg, just the shell was left. Maybe the deads were bein' pushed into them eggs and hatchin' out. This must be some kind of special bird; Lt. Dan said it must be an Angel bird. Sergeant Ray said it probably made its nest right on the ground so the people in the ground could get in it easier. Now they were pretty sure, when you die you get the dirt sandwich. Then your new job is to push the daisies up through the ground. Then, if you do a good daisy pushin' job.

You get pushed into one of them eggs and turn into a bird. Now they knew why Ole Commander was happy when he went up. Low Heaven is right there where the birds fly. The Field Marshall was pretty smart, she musta have known what they were lookin' for and led em to it.

Ben said; so you die then turn into a bird, and go to Low heaven. Dan said; when you double die you go back to pushin' daisies, and then get shot out of the ground, to High Heaven. They agreed you have to turn into a bird first, cause they are smaller and easier to shoot up to High Heaven. They get shot out of the ground, and put their wings back and go straight up like a rocket. That's why the ground was sunk on top of some of them graves. That's one of them people that finished their daisy pushin' early, probably somebody young. Young people that die didn't get much time to have fun, so the Angel gets them out quicker. The ground didn't even have time to settle.

Now they are flyin' around somewhere in Low Heaven, or they may have already double died and got shot to High Heaven. The Rebels had been thinkin', if you had to be in one of them heavens the high one would be best.

Everything just kinda came together. They knew what they had been lookin' for had just been spelled out. Their new discovery made em feel good; the deads that belonged to them had been there long enough they had to be past Low Heaven and already moved to High Heaven.

It only works if you have been "Bath Tized" and get doused in "Holy Water". If you ain't been "Bath Tized" you would have to push fifty or sixty more daisies before you got pushed in an egg. Unless it was one of them young people, cause they couldn't choose to get "Bath Tized", they would get a pass to get in an early egg. This was an amazin' discovery the Rebels continued their discussion. They figured that "Zombie" "Ole Gabe" fought before, musta got pushed into a rotten bird egg. He couldn't turn into a bird inside a rotten egg, that's why he stayed in the man form. It also splains where the poison Zombie death gas came from. The "deep in the cave growl" was that rotten egg makin' its way out as poison gas. The Rebels figured Zombies had to be recycled, cause of that rotten egg problem. They knew now why Zombies bury their self head first. They back into one of them eggs second time around.

They can tap it with their toe and find out if it is rotten, before they go in. No sense makin' the same mistake twice. Then they remembered that broken egg lyin' by that dip in the ground where the Zombie dug in. Maybe that Zombie backed into that egg and is flyin' around in Low Heaven right now.

Corporal Ben was wonderin' out loud; about good eggs, and bad eggs. Either way, if you get into a good egg or you get into a bad egg, you still would like to eat grubs! Zombies like em and birds do to.

They all agreed; and figured it was because all they had to eat inside that egg was the yoke. It made sense, egg yolks are mushy and grub guts are mushy. Both birds and Zombies must have a taste for mushy stuff. They probably would like eggs better, but they would have to fight for an egg. Grubs are free, just gotta dig em up.

They figured, even though you might have to fight a Zombie you should still show respect. It might be somebody you know that just got pushed into the wrong egg. Heck; that Zombie probably don't feel good about it either. But that don't mean you should just let em suck on your brain.

If they was of their normal self and knew how freaky they was, they wouldn't want somebody to just hand over a brain. Specially a good friend or family. Course, they would probably spect a good friend or family to be nice and least give em a little whiskey.

They would have to wait to get to High Heaven before they found out how to get to Universe Heaven. They wondered how the Field Marshall was gonna act when she can't find Ole Commander. The Rebels would be forced to tell her; he probably ran off after some girl chicken. Or he got ate up by one of them "screamin hissers", or some other critter. Private Jack said, "Ole Commander" could be pushin' up daisies and it won't be long before he really can fly right up there in "Low Heaven".

Private Pig said, Heck Ole Commander and that Zombie fella might be tellin' war stories to each other about the fights they had with the Rebels. They all agreed, even though the Rebels didn't like him at first the Ole Korean Commander" turned out to be one tough warrior. And that Zombie musta been pretty tough to take out "Ole Gabe". The Rebels weren't sure about forgivin' him just yet.

After all "Ole Gabe" was their good friend. Come to think of it "Ole Gabe ought to be about done with his daisy pushin'.

Lt. Dan said he was sure, "Ole Gabe" with a brand new body, bird or not. He was gonna wallop that Zombie.

The Squawk Hoppers and Angels Choir

It was getting to be fall and the Rebels were hanging out after dark. The air was still, and they kept hearing something that sounded like singing. They wandered around the compound trying to figure out where that sound was coming from. They got to the north side of headquarters and it sounded like it was coming from over the hill in the shallow pond. This was gonna be an excellent adventure. The Rebels were back and ready for some excitement. Lt. Dan said o.k. boys; this can't be as sloppy as the "Screamin Hisser" fight. We are professionals, and we need to act like it. Corporal Ben said, I thought that fight was pretty darn professional; I got the brain scars to prove it. Lt. Dan said, heck we didn't even find out what in the world we were even fightin'. Corporal Ben said, all I'm sayin' is the dang thing was meaner than all the other critters we fought, and we won. Does it matter what it was? Dan said, we need to be able to recognize our enemy in case we have to fight it again.

The Rebels eased down by the shallow pond.

They could hear the singing now, first right in front of them, then across on the other bank. Whatever it was they were singing to each other. They eased forward, suddenly a squawk and a splash. They looked to see what it was. Just a small pair of eyes; sittin' on the water. Singin', floating eyes, this was strange. They heard the Field Marshall calling, so they lit out for headquarters.

Lt. Dan said; those eyes got to be connected to somethin'. I didn't see a mouth on them eyes. How are they singin'?

The Next morning the Rebels started planning their night time adventure. They were out doing chores, but they could hear them squawkers down at the shallow pond. Lt. Dan said we need to find out what's going on with those squawkin eyes. The Field Marshall called them in, she said after dinner you need to get in those beds and stay there. The Rebels went to their barracks. Lt. Dan said short nap boys, we're goin' out tonight. They kept their clothes on, Lt. Dan shook them awake. They slipped across the hall; they need to make sure they closed that window. Those girls made enough noise when they slept.

If they all got colds it would probably sound like the "Mud Sliders" were sleepin' in there.

The Rebels got down on the ground and lit out for the shallow pond. They could hear those squawkers singin'. The Rebels slipped over the bank of the pond, look said Lt. Dan. He pointed at those floatin' eyes in the middle of the pond. The Rebels slipped around the edge of the pond tryin' to keep from getting' wet and muddy. The Field Marshal would know they had gone out if they came back all muddy. Lt. Dan held out his arm to stop the other Rebels. He pointed toward somethin' on the bank. He picked up a mud clod and chunked it over there. A squawk, and a hop then whatever it was disappeared.

The eyes popped up on the water. Man, this is weird! O.K. everybody pick up somethin' to throw. The Rebels picked up whatever they could find. Lt. Dan said; now Ben I want you to throw over there when I say throw. Jack you over there, Pig over there and Ray over there. I will throw over to the far end. Ready, Throw. The Rebels threw whatever they had, then a bunch of squawks and splashes. Then; eyes on the water everywhere. Private Jack said look! There it was; a "frog".

That's what those things are; we are gonna have a "Holy Frog War" shouted Private Pig. Shhh! Lt. Dan had to shush him so they wouldn't be noticed.

They live in that water, so they are the same as "Bath Tized" said Lt. Dan. The Old Lord probably needs a few up there in High Heaven, or maybe even Universe Heaven. Corporal Ben added; who knows, there may be a big demand for these singin' hoppers when the Angels sing up on high. Like that song they had to sing at church. They may use these fellas for the Angels choir. Lt. Dan said it's settled; we will send a few on their way, if there ain't no complaints we will send some more. We are liable to get a big shiny star right up there to look at just for makin' "Old Lord" happy. They decided; just to be safe the Rebels would confess their sins, so they would get a good clean start.

They had been told the "Old Family" was of the "Cat Lick" religion, they had been big on that "Holy Water", "Bath Tizin", and Confessin' sin. The Rebels didn't like the idea of lickin a cat, but sacrifices have to be made sometimes.

The next day after the Rebels were finished with their duties, they lit out in search of a cat. Private Jack finally caught one; it acted and sounded a lot like one of those "Screamin' Hissers". The Rebels gathered around in a circle. Lt. Dan started the services. He licked the cat and passed it to Sergeant Ray; Ray got his lick and passed it to Ben. This continued until every Rebel had licked the cat. The cat really seemed to like it. They all spat on the ground and used their shirt sleeves to drag the hair off their tongues. Cats don't taste very good. Maybe if it was fried it would be better.

They had never heard of that, and didn't have time to think on it right now. Let that thing go said Lt. Dan. Alright who's gonna confess first? They all looked around at each other, nobody volunteered. Lt. Dan said alright then; I will make the decision. Corporal Ben! Go first! Ben bowed his head and placed his hand over his heart. He took a deep breath and said, "Old Lord", I am sorry I was mean to Ole Commander. And I am sorry I decapitated them chickens, even though the Field Marshall says she ain't gonna cook em with the head on. And "Old Lord" I'm sorry for any cursin, spittin and any general meanness, I'm pretty sure, I done.

Lt. Dan said that about covers it. Then Lt. Dan said "Old Lord" us other four feels the same way. Now! To get square and right with ya "Old Lord". Corporal Ben is gonna say "Hail Mary". Ben raised his head up but kept his hand over his heart and said, Hail Mary, with a pocket full of Grace" forgive us our trespassin and chase that Devil away. That's the way the Rebels understood you have to say it. If you was sneakin around on somebody's land you had to confess so. The Rebels surely wouldn't want somebody sneakin around their fortress! And they were about to do some sneakin around. This way they could get a pass from "Old Lord" hisself! Well any way you have to put "Grace" in there, cause they had heard the Ole Preacher man say "The Devil and Grace Do Not Mix".

It took a while for the Rebels to figure the Hail Mary thing out. What you do is say that verse. Then Hail Mary takes some of that Grace out of her pocket and mixes it with water and freezes it up to make hail. Then she throws that down at the Ole Devil.

Well the Devil bein' so hot and not likin all that ice cold hail full of "Grace". He cools his heels pretty darn quick.

So right away he heads for his oven, cause he figures that "Grace" will get him if he's to cool. Cause when he's cool he slows way down, kinda like that lava stuff. The only thing left to do was make a cross on their foreheads before the start of the war. They could use pond mud for that, after all this was a Christian kindness they were fixin to perform.

It's not every day a person gets to help out the angels up on high. If you fight the war you have to wear the symbol. A cross should about do it. Well time to sneak back in, "The Holy Frog War" starts tomorrow night. The next day the Rebels hurried through their duties, they had weapon preparations to make. The Rebels took a cane pole and tied a string to the end. Then they screwed a screen door eye into the side of the pole. They ran the string through the eye and made a loop then back through the eye. They should be able to slide the pole out over a frog, drop the loop over its head and then pull the string.

The Rebels went out the window and down to the shallow pond. They slipped up over the bank, and up to the water's edge. Lt. Dan said stick your finger in the mud and follow what I do.

The Rebels all stuck their finger in the mud, then Lt. Dan said in the name of the "Father, the Son and Holy Smoke". Us Christian Coal Town Rebels hereby representin the angels up on high make a cross on our head. We hereby pledge to send the finest singers to the angel's choir. We vow to not curse, swear or blast a femur in line of our duly sworn job. They put that blast a femur in there; cause they heard "Ole Preacher" say "No one can be a blast a femur and a proper Christian".

The Rebels knew all about that blast part, they did plenty of that tryin' to find Mike. Lt. Dan said he found out in health class a femur was a big ole leg bone.

Well, the Rebels surely couldn't represent the angels with a blasted, broke leg bone; so it made sense not to do it. Then all the Rebels made their cross on their foreheads. No doubt now, they was gonna bless these frogs with eternal singin. Lt Dan said enough ceremony it's time to send some hoppers on their way. There's one, try out that hoop pole Lt. Dan said.

Ray slipped the pole out over the frogs head. Then he dropped the loop and pulled back until the string was close to the frog's croaker.

Ray was excited, he jerked the string and the frog said "RRRUUUPPP". Ray jerked the pole up at the same time and the frog went way up in the air behind em. The Rebels looked around in time to see that frog bounce off the windshield of a pickup truck going down the road. "Oh Crud" said Lt. Dan, we got to be careful we are close to the road. If anybody sees us out here we will catch heck. Maybe whoever was in that truck didn't notice anything? It was funny seein' that frog fly away though. It's not every day a person gets to see a flyin' frog!

They continued to use the hoop pole to sling frogs up in the air and away from the pond. It was getting' late and Lt. Dan said it was time to sneak back in.

The next morning, they had finished their morning chores and were having breakfast. "Ole Frank" the neighbor from up the hill came visiting. He was talking to the Field Marshall. He said that crazy brother of mine! He said he was drivin down the road over the hill there, and it started rainin frogs. The Field Marshall said "I have never heard of such a thing". "Old Frank" said me neither; I think he had too much to drink. The Rebels excused themselves so they could go outside. The Field Marshall said o.k., but I want you to wash that mud off your heads. How in the world did all of you get mud on your heads in the same place?

Lt. Dan said; we was lookin through them boards where we feed the Ogre's , must have been some mud on them. Well it probably ain't mud then the Field Marshall said. Get your nasty heads washed!

There she goes bein all serious again. They sure didn't want the Field Marshall to find out, they was makin that frog rain.

The Rebels did their duties as quick as they could, days were getting shorter and they didn't have much time left after chores to get stuff ready. They decided they would make a couple more of those hoop poles. When they were finished they went inside, they needed a nap before going out tonight.

Later that night the Rebels slipped across the hall and dropped down on the porch. They grabbed their poles and turned to jump off the porch. "Oh Holy Crud" the Field Marshall was standing there with her hands on her hips. I figured you nuts were sneaking out somehow, she said. Just where do you think you're going? Lt. Dan said well we was gonna do some late night fishin'. Does it have anything to do with frogs? She asked. Lt. Dan said; nah not really, well maybe for bait. We just thought maybe we could do some fishin'; we don't get to go very often. Then a surprise! The Field Marshall smiled and said; well don't stay out all night, you still have chores tomorrow. They weren't sure but they thought they heard her laughin when she was walkin back to headquarters.

Then they heard her say "raining frogs", and they really heard her laugh that time. The rebels headed for the shallow pond, they were ready for some serious frog slingin'. Them angels was probably wonderin if they were gonna get any more help. The second wave shoulda already been on its way.

The next morning the Field Marshall woke them and said get your breakfast. Old Lil up the road doesn't want to feed chickens this winter. She wants us to come and take them off her hands.

The Rebels climbed in the pickup after breakfast. Ray, Jack and Pig got in the back and Dan and Ben got in the cab. The Field Marshall was driving; she turned on the road beside the shallow pond. Right there hanging from a branch of a tree was a dead frog. Brother they were gonna get it now! The Rebels knew she was gonna punish em. Then there on the road! "Dead Frog". The Field Marshall looked over at Dan and Ben and said maybe that old man wasn't too drunk! Dan said maybe! Ben just kept his head down, his head had healed up a while back, and he wasn't askin to get no "pop knots" on it.

It was getting cold and the shallow pond had frozen over, it had been a month since the Rebels sent the singing hoppers to the Angels Choir. So far; not one Rebel had been struck dead by God. And they hadn't gotten in trouble, by the Field Marshall. Now they were just gonna set back and enjoy the winter. It was dark and snowin'; the Rebels were pretty sure school was gonna be cancelled.

They asked the Field Marshall if they could go out and mess around in the snow. Go ahead, but don't stay out too late, she said. The Rebels tossed a few snow balls around; it's fun to dodge snow balls in the dark. Then Lt. Dan looked up. He said take a look boys. There it was! A big bright star that looked like it was above the shallow pond to the north. Lt. Dan said "Old Lord" likes that choir.

Who Dan Pollock Chicken Disease

The Rebels managed to stay out of trouble through spring and it was getting to be summer. They had been surprised when they got to Ole Lil's to pickup those chickens. When they walked into the chicken coop Lt. Dan said; them are some weird lookin chickens!

Ole Lil said they're "Who Dan" (Houdan). Lt. Dan said I don't know! Lil said; No them chickens are "Who Dan"! Lt. Dan said I don't know! Ole Lil said no I mean they are "Who Dan". Lt. Dan looked at Corporal Ben and shrugged. He rolled his eyes and pointed his thumb over his shoulder at Ole Lil. When they got outside, Lt. Dan said I think she got crazy, she don't even know them's chickens. Why have chickens; if ya don't know what they are and why ya got em? She needs a doctor if she has to ask neighbors about her own chickens. I was waitin for her to say "Who Ben" then you could say I don't know! They got a good laugh out of that. Lt. Dan said he thought her marble had a crack in it. Since moving the chickens to their coop they had gone through winter and spring without any real problems.

But, they had been keeping an eye on em anyway. Lt. Dan asked the Field Marshall about Ole Lil and them chickens. He said why did Ole Lil keep sayin Who Dan? The Field Marshall said because those chickens are Who Dan. Lt. Dan said I don't know? The Field Marshall said; no they are Who Dan. Lt. Dan said I don't know, but they look Pollock to me!

The Field Marshall said that's right they're Who Dan! Lt. Dan said; Pollock! The Field Marshall said right! Lt. Dan went out of headquarters more confused than before. Corporal Ben saw him and asked; what's the matter with you?

Lt. Dan said; best I can tell we are strapped with a bunch of dumb Pollock's that don't know they's chickens and everybody's expecting me to find out why .When I tell em they's Pollock, they act like they forget again, right away and ask me who they are evertime they decide to talk about em. Corporal Ben said; well maybe they got that amnesia thing. Lt. Dan said the squat trots won't make you lose your memory. That's just somethin Colonel Jim used to say to be funny. Ben said; what in the world are you talkin about? Lt. Dan said you know when he would say he squatted so hard he got amnesia.

Corporal Ben said well maybe he did! He wasn't all that good at figurin out who we was fightin, you're a lot better! Jim was better at whackin chickens than makin plans on how to whack em! Ben said you don't know maybe he got some kind of chicken disease that made him squat. He may have got his memory gone from chicken disease and thought it was squattin! Is it possible to squat your memory gone? Lt. Dan said you got me, but let's make sure we don't squat that hard! How do you know how hard to squat? Lt. Dan said if your ears feel hot that's too hard! Lt. Dan said; we did enough talkin about squattin.

Why do you think them chickens, the Field Marshall and Ole Lil don't know who them chickens are? Corporal Ben said; well I said it before! Maybe it's some kind o chicken disease! Lt. Dan said; well chickens are dumb, but all the others we had before least knew they was chickens! I bet it's somethin to do with em bein Pollock. Ben said maybe, but it's gonna be tough to find out. Lt. Dan said well we need to build our meetin place!

So they busied themselves building a meeting place. This way they could have privacy when they had Rebel business to discuss.

They had picked out the tallest tree in the field. They had already built climbing steps and were putting the floor in place. The Field Marshall called them in, it was time for supper, then get ready for bed. The Rebels thought all that sleeping was a waste, but the Field Marshall had cut off every escape attempt. So what could they do? Just go ahead and waste that time sleeping.

The next morning the Field Marshall said; after breakfast, I want that chicken coop cleaned out. And check to see if them hens are laying yet! Man! They had been avoidin' cleanin' that nasty chicken dirt for a long time. Who knows what kind of sickness they could catch from them Pollock chickens. As soon as the Rebels walked into the coop, here come the bony Pollock. He looked like one of them dusters the girls used in headquarters. Just a bunch of feathers on a stick. Dan walked toward him, he was tryin' to look into his eye.

That's the best way to find out if a chicken was thinkin' or not. Most of the time a chicken just don't think. Ya decapitate one and another will run right to it. All you gotta do is grab it, and he's next in line. You would think they would run away if they had a brain.

Once they run up there; they ain't gonna have a brain for long! Lt. Dan was circlin' Ole Bony. Then Private Jack said gee's look at the size of that egg! The Rebels all looked, there was a huge white egg. Lt. Dan said maybe it is possible to squat your memory gone. Them chickens ain't that big but that egg is. Lt. Dan said alright boy's run these Pollock's out; so's we can clean out their nasty dirt! The Rebels ran the chickens out and cleaned the coop. Private Pig came running up with a box under his arm. Lt. Dan said what's in the box? Pig opened it up; cigars!

Lt. Dan said we are done boys head for the fort. The Rebels climbed into the fort and Pig passed around the cigars.

They lit em up and started puffin away. They felt big puffin on them cigars. Then Lt. Dan said does anybody else feel funny? The other Rebels were all saggy eyed and dizzy. Corporal Ben said I got a gopher in my belly, Jack said me too, Pig said he had bubbles in his neck, Ray said me to. They heard Lt. Dan say; "Old Lord please save us from Pollock Chicken Disease". They were sure them chickens had poisoned them with Pollock Chicken Disease.

Lt. Dan told; Corporal Ben to do some of that Bible Talkin and maybe Old Lord would save em. Corporal Ben said I don't know no Bible Talkin that covers Pollock Chicken Disease. Lt. Dan said well say somethin from the bible before we die! Corporal Ben said alright then. He forced himself up, closed his left eye and looked at the top of the tree. He sat there lookin' for a moment; then he put his hand on his heart, and looked up to high heaven. "Exit Us, one, three, dot top a dot, two and five". (Exodus 13:25) Worship Old LORD, and his blessin will be on your food and water. I will take away sickness from amongst ya. They all said "AMEN"! Lt. Dan said it must be workin, I already feel better. He said don't forget that bible talkin we may need it again! And get rid of them cigars, they must be settin that Pollock Chicken Disease off. The Rebels still felt a little wobbly so they decided to get their evening chores done and call it a day.

The next morning before breakfast the Field Marshall said go get me some eggs from the chicken coop. Lt. Dan and Corporal Ben went and gathered eggs.

The Field Marshall said; my Lord those are the biggest chicken eggs I ever saw!

The Rebels were surprised cause they figured she was friends with that Ole Man Moses. If the Field Marshall; had never seen eggs that big as old as she was. Then them chickens definitely squatted their memory gone. The Rebels decided they was gonna help them chickens get their memory back!

They opened the coop and the chickens started walkin' out. That dumb lookin' head straight up and their chest stuck out. They would stick one leg straight out and set it down and then the other leg straight out and set it down. They looked like they was marchin' out of that coop. The Pollock's walked out and stood in front of the Rebels, lookin' down their beak at em. Private Pig said they make ya want a whack em a good one don't they? Lt. Dan said that's part of the problem they have! Yesterday they was Pollock's and today they are Scotland Yard Police! I was right these chickens are seriously confused!

The Rebels decided to watch the chickens for a few days and see how they acted each day.

Lt. Dan said them chickens are squattin their memory gone ever time they lay one of them big eggs.

Catch one and bring it here. Private Jack caught a Pollock and took it to Dan. Dan took a small board and put on the chickens backside. Then he stretched a rubber band and looped it over the chicken's leg, then the other leg and across the board. He pulled it up over the chicken's thighs. There said Lt. Dan; that will hold that egg in, so that one will know it's a chicken tomorrow!

The next day the Rebels beat it out to the coop to let the Pollock's out. They just walked out and acted like the Rebels didn't exist. Private Jack said; well today they's just snobs! The Ole feather stick walked over and stood next to Lt. Dan. Dan said well this Ole Pollock likes us anyways! Maybe he is the only one that knows who he is! Lt. Dan said wait; where's the one with the board? The Rebels looked in the coop. The Pollock with the board was standin' on the nest with it's neck stickin' straight out. Lt. Dan said look it's froze like a statue.

Ben walked up and the chicken didn't move, Ben raised the head feathers up. The chickens eyes looked like they belonged on one of them tunnel rats. It's beak was open but nothin' was comin' out and it's head skin was all red! Lt. Dan said take that board off; Ben took the board off. Then a egg fell out of that chicken and it let out a squawk and unfroze. Ben turned it loose and it ran out in the pen. That dumb Pollock squawked for an hour!

This was a new discovery for the Rebels. They never knew they had the power to freeze chickens into statues by blockin' that egg from comin' out.

The Rebels weren't sure if it was better to keep the egg in or go ahead and let the chicken squat it out. That one sure made a lot of noise when they let it out. And it still acted confused! Oh well, maybe if you want to keep them chickens quiet, just board em up! It sure would make it easier to catch em. But you would have to catch em to board em up anyway's. The Ole Pollock started followin' em around where ever they went. He really liked Lt. Dan and Corporal Ben. They always dug up worms and gave to him. Lt. Dan figured it was time to do somethin' about those confused chickens. The board and rubber band wasn't gonna work, unless they wanted statue chickens. He called the Rebels together. He said ya know if we was to scare some feathers off them Pollocks maybe they'll remember they's chickens.

Lt. Dan said I don't wanna do it cause the Field Marshall might catch us. Sergeant Ray said what are we gonna do? Lt. Dan said send the 1st Mechanized Artillery Squad in there. They can scare chickens better than we can!

The Rebels brought the Artillery Squad over and sent them in the pen.

They chased the Chickens around and around the pen, finally Lt. Dan said that's enough. Now we wait and see how they act in the mornin'. The next morning the Rebels opened the coop. The Pollock's bolted out of the coop and Ole board butt was in the lead. The Pollock's just kept running. Lt. Dan said they're still confused, they think they're marathon runners now! Lt. Dan asked Ben do ya know any more of that bible talkin? Corporal Ben said how is bible talkin gonna help them chickens, know they's chickens? Lt. Dan said well I don't know but give it a go and we'll see!

Corporal Ben squinted his left eye shut and looked up at the willow tree. Lt. Dan said whatcha lookin for?

Ben said I'm readin my brain to see if I can find some of that bible talkin! Then Ben put his hand over his heart, Lt. Dan said ya found one didn't ya? Corporal Ben looked up to High Heaven and said; Mark, one, dot top a dot, four and zero. (Mark 1:40) A man with a "Leopard, Z" came to him beggin' on his knees, If you are willin', ya can make me clean.

Lt. Dan said that was not any bible talkin' to help chickens! They ain't Leopard Z's and how does a Z get to be a Leopard?

And who cares if they's clean? Ya need to find one to fix their stupid! Corporal Ben said well; I told ya, they was no bible talkin' to help chickens! Lt. Dan said; I don't think ya tried all that hard!

Ben said; I didn't read my whole brain; I just read last Sunday's part! Lt. Dan said well give it another look; Ben said why don't ya read your own brain and find one.

Lt. Dan said I don't want my brain all cluttered up; that's how I can think of how to fix problems. Dan said; go ahead give it another look! Ben squinted his eye and looked up at the willow tree. The other Rebels came over and all of em started looking up in the tree. Private Jack said; what we lookin at? Lt. Dan said shhh, he's readin his brain! Private Pig said; how do ya read a brain. Lt. Dan said shhh! It's a gift, I only ever seen him do it! Private Jack asked; did he get it for Christmas or his birthday? Lt. Dan said; I think Old Lord gave it to him. Private Pig asked; when was Old Lord here anyway's? Lt. Dan said; Ole Preacher says he's here all the time. Sergeant Ray said; well I ain't seen him. Lt. Dan said me neither!

Then Ben put his hand over his heart. Lt. Dan said; see he got one! Sergeant Ray said; what did he get? Dan said; shhh, it's Bible talkin! Private Pig said; how ya get Bible Talkin writ in your brain? Lt. Dan said shhh, I told ya it's a gift!

 Ben looked up to High heaven and said; James, five, dot top a dot, one and three! (James 5:13). Is anyone amongst ya sufferin? Let him pray. Lt. Dan said that's it? That's the best ya can do? Corporal Ben said; it's gonna have to do! They ain't nothin writ in there past last Thursday, but some home work and pitchers of me whackin chickens and slingin frogs! Lt. Dan said; let's give it up, and check on them Pollock's again tomorrow. The next mornin the Rebels opened the coop and the chickens acted like normal chickens. Lt. Dan said that Bible Talkin must work for chickens to!

The Rebels went into headquarters for breakfast and the Field Marshall said; how are those "Who Dan" chickens? Lt. Dan said; **I don't know**! After breakfast Lt. Dan said well we got them chickens fixed. The people will have to figure out them's chickens, for their self! All I know I'm tired of sayin I don't know.

Floozy Chicken Female Disgrace

The Field Marshall decided to keep the Pollock chickens cause she liked them big eggs. Everybody quit asking Lt. Dan who them chickens was and just started calling em Pollock's. They reckoned them people fixed they selves, and didn't forget anymore; them was just chickens. The Rebels were getting bored since they bible talked the confusion out of them chickens. Now they were just hanging around with nothing to do and it was getting to be fall. The summer adventures would be over soon. Now in the evenings they would do chores and sit on the porch waiting for something, heck they would take anything at this point. Lt. Dan said; I can't take one more day of this, tomorrow we do somethin'!

The next day they talked about maybe catching some of them chickens and boardin' em up. Then they talked about paintin' em different colors as a surprise for the Field Marshall. Bring a little color into the compound. Heck she liked all the colorful flowers in the spring, they could give her early color and she would get a double dose. Get some now and spring to, she would probably like that. Lt. Dan said what if we painted the Ogre's, the Mud Slider's and them Pollock's? Ben said; nah where would we get that much paint? Lt. Dan said I reckon that's right! Let's go in and see if we can find any paintin' stuff.

The Rebels went inside headquarters and looked around; there wasn't anything they could use in sight.

Lt. Dan said I know they's some paint in the basement. They took off to have a look. They found some white paint and some brown. Lt Dan said; that wasn't gonna be very colorful. Then Private Pig came in, he had a small bottle. Lt. Dan asked; what did ya find?

Pig held it up; it was what them girls put on their fingernails! Bright red, Lt. Dan said they ain't enough of that, to paint even one chicken. Corporal Ben said; it don't take much to paint fingers I guess. Lt. Dan said; well fingernails and chicken beaks is bout the same! Let's get us a Pollock and paint its beak, least that will help color things a little. Private Jack caught a Pollock; Jack was alway's best at catchin' chickens. Lt Dan painted the chicken's beak and turned it loose. Sergeant Ray said look! How come that chicken's staggerin' around?

  Lt. Dan said; it musta got fumed, this stuff stinks! Let's get another one, that's kinda funny! The Rebels painted till dark, they had used all the paint, but they got all of the chickens. Them chickens was probably gonna sleep good tonight. They looked like a bunch of drunks. They wasn't even sittin' on the roost they was layin' on their sides with their head and neck hangin' off. The Rebels went inside for supper and sleeping time.

  The next morning the Rebels let the chickens out of the coop, Jack said they all look like they're wearin' that lip paint them girls use. Lt. Dan said; say we need to get us some of that. Pig, go see if ya can find some of that lip paint.

Pig was best at sneakin' in and getting' stuff. Lt. Dan said we need some of that white paint from the basement. Corporal Ben took off to get the white paint. When Pig and Ben got back Lt. Dan told Jack to catch one of them Pollock's. Jack came back with a Pollock; Ben said I thought you said that white paint wasn't very colorful! Lt. Dan said; don't be interruptin' when I got my brain workin'. I don't interrupt you when you're bible talkin'! This is why I don't clutter my brain up with all that writin', and if ya just be quiet; I'll splain it.

Lt. Dan said O.K. them chickens are mostly black. So what we got to do is paint stripes on their head feathers. Then we will use that lip paint on their backside. The Rebels painted away. It took longer to put the stripes on than it took to dob that lip paint on their butts. When they were finished Dan told Pig, to put that lip paint back exactly where he found it. They cleaned up the mess and shut the chickens up, after church tomorrow the Field Marshall was sure gonna be surprised!

They all got in the car the next morning to go to church. The Field Marshall kept making sour faces, they figured she must of got up in a bad move. The Field Marshall told em before "once in a while people just get up in a bad move". They figured she musta fell out of bed; that surely would be a bad move. After church they got back home, and the Field Marshall yelled What in God's name is the matter with them chickens.

Man! she really did get up in a bad move. Lt. Dan said they ain't nothin' wrong with em, we just painted em up so's you could see some pretty colors!

The Field Marshall said exactly what; is that on their butts? Lt. Dan said that's some of that lip paint, but we didn't use all of it. We put it back exactly where we found it. The Field Marshall really got mad! She said that's my lipstick; no wonder I kept smelling something terrible all morning, I'm gonna skin all of you. She said there will be no more chicken painting and leave other peoples stuff alone.

The Rebels bailed out of the car, they sure didn't want a skinning. The Field Marshall stomped into headquarters. Lt. Dan said man ya try to do good and look what happens. Then they heard a crack, that lip paint hit Lt. Dan right in the back of the head.

Corporal Ben said; well did that unclutter your brain? Ya didn't get skinned, I think she added some skin; lookin' at that pop knot! Can I touch it? Lt. Dan said; no it's sore and just keep it up, your skinnin' may still happen.

Lt. Dan said; let's get out of these church clothes, we can surely find somethin' to do that won't make the Field Marshall mad. The Rebels hurried to get those church clothes off and get into their feeling good clothes. Them church clothes always felt itchy.

The time had come to get rid of a few of them "Who Dan's". The Field Marshall said she didn't want too many laying hens, they was too many eggs. She said they might make good bakin' hens.

The Rebels weren't sure how you could turn a hen into bacon. They were pretty sure bacon came from them Mud Slider's. Maybe the Field Marshall was losin' her mind, heck she could have that Pollock Chicken Disease and don't know it!

Or she mighta banged her noggin when she fell outta bed, during that bad move. Whatever it was they would keep an eye on her; right now though they were up for a little action. Lt. Dan said what about Ole Pollock? We kinda like him!

The Field Marshall said; well I think we can keep him around for a little while. He's probably gonna be too tough anyway. The Rebels had already figured Ole Pollock was gonna be tough. Besides likin' him they weren't so sure they wanted to fight him. The Field Marshall said alright then first thing in the morning we will get busy. Good! The Rebels had hoped there would be a little time to make war preparations.

Lt. Dan said alright we need to come up with some new weapeeens. The last of that word was high pitch like a girl. Corporal Ben said what in the world are you talkin' about? Lt. Dan's face turned red and he said I didn't mean to say it that way! Ben said oh! Just a slip of the tongue then? Lt. Dan said yea. Corporal Ben was worried about him; he had been making funny noises when he talked. He also noticed Lt. Dan was starting to act goofy when one of them girls brought their friends around.

That Pollock Chicken Disease mighta got in his blood or somethin'. There might be little Pollock germs swimmin' around in his blood right now.

Corporal Ben said you probably don't know it, but you might have Pollock germs swimmin' in your blood.

Let me cut you a little bit and we will take a look to see if anythin' is in there. Lt. Dan said get away from me you idiot. You're not gonna cut me and there ain't nothin' in my blood. Corporal Ben said O.K. but I want you to know I'm here. I won't; let nothin' destroy your brain! The Rebels went about designing new weapons; Lt. Dan never said a thing. Corporal Ben was thinking about them old frog slingers from when they had been helping the Angels up on high. The same thing might work on them Pollock's.

After all they couldn't see all that well with that junk over their eyes, and you could reach a long ways with that pole. Ben told Dan; Lt. Dan said yea.

That's it? You ain't gonna say nothin' but yea? Lt. Dan walked off. Corporal Ben couldn't believe he just walked out on weapon preparations!

The other Rebels were worried about Dan to. They decided to find out what was bothering him. Weapons can wait; they would just use the old ones. The rebels took off chasing Dan. He went into headquarters. During the day when he could be outside? Somethin' was definitely wrong! The Rebels snuck inside. They could hear talkin'. They slipped up closer; it was the Field Marshall and Lt. Dan. The Field Marshall said it's not anything to worry about! Your voice is just changing.

All young people go through this thing called puberty! The Rebels looked at each other; then slipped back outside. Sergeant Ray said man I hope my voice don't do that.

I surely don't want to squeal around like a girl. Corporal Ben said that's enough talkin' about my brother. Lt. Dan will be alright he's just got a little problem right now.

The Rebels finished gathering their weapons in anticipation of tomorrow's event. Lt. Dan should be O.K. by then and they would get back to business. The next morning after breakfast the Rebels were ready to get on with the business at hand. It really wasn't gonna be much of a war, there aren't that many of those Pollock's.

The Rebels slipped down by the chicken coop. Private Pig said there are a few in the pen, Private Jack said there are several in the coop.

Ben said, the Field Marshall only wants to keep fifteen. Alright we will move in and eliminate the ones in the pen. Sergeant Ray said; I will slip over by the coop and slam the door while you guys go after the snobs in the pen. Then we will let all but fifteen out and keep the ones in the coop. Corporal Ben looked around for Lt. Dan. There he was just sittin' over there on a log. Usually Lt. Dan was makin' all the plans and everything went good. Corporal Ben called a time out and said I will be right back. He slipped over by Lt. Dan and sat on the log beside him. He asked Dan what's up? Are you comin' over to help us fight? Lt. Dan said no, I will help after the war is over.

Then Ben noticed Lt. Dan lookin' off toward the front of headquarters. A girl! Corporal Ben asked; are you lookin' at that girl? Lt. Dan said no! But she is pretty.

Old Lord; have mercy Corporal Ben said! You are more interested in lookin' at that dumb ole girl than you are fightin' chickens? Lt. Dan said shut up you big dummy, she might hear you. Corporal Ben said well we are gonna fight this war with you or without you. Lt. Dan said go ahead! Corporal Ben said alright but you need to unscramble your brain.

Girls are girls; they're clean and have long finger nails with no dirt under em and they smell funny! I'm goin back to the important stuff! Corporal Ben slipped back down to the pen.

The Rebels attacked the Pollock's in the pen then attacked the others that Ray let out of the coop. It seemed like a meaningless fight, the Pollock's surely weren't fighters. Even the Ole Pollock jumped on a few and they never put up much of a fight. Dan helped with the cleaning and putting the hens in the freezer.

Ben was waiting for an opportunity to catch him away from the others so they could talk. Finally a chance to talk! Corporal Ben asked, so whats really goin' on? Lt. Dan said I'm not interested in chicken wars or any other kind of war. Corporal Ben said Old Lord is gonna Blast A Femur on you talkin' like that! I don't care if you get eat up with Pooperty, ya don't turn your back on the Rebels. Lt. Dan said I ain't worried about Pooperty or a Blast A Femur, and walked off.

This ain't right, maybe tomorrow will be better. Lt. Dan may have a sickness! Corporal Ben remembered when he had the squat trots and he didn't feel like fightin' or talkin'.

Maybe that was it. Lt Dan probably had squat trots. That should be gone by tomorrow!

The next morning the Rebels went out to do chores and Lt. Dan seemed to be talking more and laughing. Corporal Ben decided he was gonna be alright now.

The sun was straight up so Ben knew it was time to eat lunch, Old Lord makes the sun burn your neck a little so ya know it's time to rest. He went into headquarters to wash up. He hadn't seen Lt. Dan since chores this morning. But he had been down by Ole Gabe's workin' on the fence. Lt. Dan was probably doin' some other kind of chore in the compound. Corporal Ben came around the corner to go into the mess hall and the Field Marshall stopped him. She said I will bring your lunch to you in the other room. Ben peeked around the corner and there was Lt. Dan sittin' with a girl havin' lunch. What a sickenin' sight! They was gigglin' and holdin' hands. Corporal Ben looked up and put his hand on his heart. Old Lord; please forgive him. He's too young to get the blast a femur.

It has to be Pollock Chicken Disease or that stinkin' girl gave him some kind of par fume poison.

Old Lord, don't let him squat hisself to death, I know the Field Marshall said he had the pooperty. That's all I'm gonna say, just remember he has been a good Christian Warrior.

Ben was confused now, how could an outstanding warrior like Lt. Dan; get all goofy over some smelly ole girl. Well he wasn't gonna figure this one out for a long time.

There was no way he was gonna fall for all that voice changin', hand holdin', bad smelly girl, giggly stuff. The next morning Lt. Dan looked different he was all happy laughin' and talkin'. Ben was thinking he might go pick him some flowers.

That ought to make him remember he's supposed to be a Rebel and forget about them dumb girls. His voice was lower now though, maybe he was getting' them swollen neck globs? Corporal Ben wasn't sure what those globs were but when they swelled up it was hard to swallow and made his voice change. That's probably what's goin' on with Lt. Dan. No need for flowers just yet, sides he wasn't sure if Lt. Dan was gonna get mad! Lt. Dan was meaner than anybody he knew when he was mad. He surely didn't wanna make him mad!

Course at this point he was willin' to take a knot or two to get Lt. Dan away from them girls. Yuk and double Yuk, the thought of them girls made his breakfast jump into his neck.

The Field Marshall announced there would only be a few chickens from now on, just a few egg laying hens and the Ole Pollock.

The other Rebels joined up with some of the younger fellas to make a new Rebel gang. Corporal Ben just lost interest; bein' a Rebel wouldn't be the same without Lt. Dan. He sat down on that log to think.

The Ole Pollock came running over and set down on the ground by him. Corporal Ben said well buddy; it looks like we are the last of the old warriors.

Then he dug a worm out of the ground with his finger and fed it to the Ole Pollock. He kept talking to Ole Pollock. Man this is unbelievable, what am I gonna do to occupy my time?

Ole Pollock stood up and hopped up on the log next to Ben. Well maybe he would go south one of these days. He surely didn't wanna go North, he heard they was fellas up there they called Yankees. Well just about one yank from one of them fella's and that fella would find out about yankin around on a retired Rebel.

Nope, probably best to not even go that way. He stood up and walked over by the chicken coop still talking to Ole Pollock. South sounded good; he heard about that southern hospitality. Well that sounded a lot like that place he had to go to get stitches once in a while. Heck them people was always nice, except maybe that one called Sister. Her whole dang family must work there, everybody in there called her sister. He heard she was a Nun, but he never knew of that family being around town. Sometimes she could be a little rough, but, she might be havin' a bad time. Ben; only ever seen her wear one outfit. She always wore that hood on her head to. Heck ya know wearin' the same clothes every day, when she took them things off; she has to be a stinker.

She probably wishes she had a few more clothes! He heard em say she was big on that Cat Lick religion.

Well she could have all that cat lickin she wants; he remembered how them cats taste, and it ain't good! Anyway's South had to be the best bet, just a few more years to go!

Then he heard a noise, he looked over and Ole Pollock was layin' on the ground. He looked up at Ben like he was confused.

Ben said; ya went to sleep and fell off the log; big dumb. I didn't do anything to ya; but maybe talk too much. Ben; squinted his left eye and looked up at the top of the willow tree. Then he put his hand on his heart and looked up to High Heaven. He said; He Brews! One, one, dot top a dot, and one. (Hebrews 11:1**)**
Now faith is the substance of things hoped for, the evidence of things not seen...

Amen!

South it is!

The End

www.ingramcontent.com/pod-product-compliance
Lightning Source LLC
Chambersburg PA
CBHW051711040426
42446CB00008B/828